Fire Your Realtor

DIY Real Estate for Everyone

Table of Contents

1: Introduction

Let me start by telling you something most people don't realize: you don't need a realtor to buy or sell property. Shocking, right? For years, we've been conditioned to believe that the only way to navigate the real estate market is by relying on professionals to do the heavy lifting. But here's the truth—buying and selling real estate is something you can absolutely do on your own. Not only is it possible, but it's also empowering, saves you money, and gives you full control over one of the biggest financial decisions of your life.

That's what this book is all about.

Now, I know what you might be thinking: "Isn't real estate complicated? Aren't there laws, contracts, and things I don't understand?" Yes, those things exist. But you don't need a fancy suit and a real estate license to figure it out. What you need is the right knowledge, a clear plan, and a little confidence to take that first step. Many people who've gone through the process on their own report feeling more in control and less pressured than those who used realtors.

And this isn't about bashing realtors. They have their place, especially when you're short on time or dealing with complex transactions. But most of the time, with the right tools and understanding, you can handle everything yourself—from pricing your home to hosting open houses and negotiating deals.

This isn't just another "how-to" guide filled with real estate jargon and complicated advice. This book is designed to be practical, hands-on, and (dare I say) fun. By the time you finish, you'll feel empowered to make smart, strategic moves, whether you're buying your first home, selling your current one, or looking to invest in properties.

You'll learn how to:
- Understand the real estate market and make sense of its ups and downs.
- Confidently search for and buy a home without feeling overwhelmed.
- Prepare, market, and sell your home like a pro.
- Handle all the legalities and paperwork that come with real estate transactions.
- Master the art of negotiation and get the best possible deal.
- Invest in real estate and start building wealth, all on your own terms.

No matter your background or experience, this book will break down everything into manageable, bite-sized steps. These chapters are packed with easy-to-follow advice, practical tips, and real-life examples from people just like you who took the DIY route.

Overall, if you have any uncertainties about the law or your rights as a consumer or homeowner, you can always mitigate risk by consulting a real estate lawyer. Although legal fees vary, the cost of hiring a lawyer might still be less than what you would pay a realtor. It's best to inquire about fees upfront to ensure you're aware of the costs involved. Consulting a lawyer where needed can provide peace of mind, helping you navigate complex processes with confidence.

Before we dive in, let's clear up a few common myths about real estate:

Myth #1: You need a realtor to find the best properties.
False. With today's online resources, you can find great properties on your own, sometimes even faster than a realtor.

Myth #2: Selling a home is too complicated for the average person.
Also false. Most of the process is straightforward, especially with the right guidance (which is exactly what you'll get here).

Myth #3: Realtors always get you a better price.
Not necessarily. While some realtors are great at negotiation, others are simply good at closing deals quickly, which doesn't always mean getting you the best price.

Myth #4: You'll get lost in the paperwork without a realtor.
You won't. Yes, there are legalities, contracts, and fine print, but I'll walk you through everything step-by-step.

Whether you're buying, selling, or investing, real estate is one of the most important financial decisions you'll ever make. And while that might sound a little daunting, it's also one of the most exciting opportunities to take control of your financial future.

This book isn't just about saving money on commissions or cutting out the middleman—it's about empowering you to make smart, confident decisions in the real estate world. You're going to learn how to read the market, negotiate like a pro, and turn real estate into a tool for building wealth, not just another stressor in your life.

So, are you ready to fire your realtor and take matters into your own hands?

Let's get started.

2: Understanding the Real Estate Market

Real estate might seem like a maze of data, jargon, and fluctuating trends, but it can be simplified. At its core, the real estate market is similar to any other market, driven by supply, demand, and timing. When more people want to buy than there are homes available, prices rise; when there's an abundance of homes and fewer buyers, prices tend to drop. By understanding these basics, you can approach your buying or selling journey with a sense of clarity and purpose.

The real estate market encompasses land and properties—from single-family homes to expansive commercial buildings. When we talk about "the market," we're referring to the ongoing buying and selling of these properties. Much like the stock market, real estate goes through cycles: times of growth, peak demand, declines, and eventual recovery. If you're in a **seller's market**, where buyers outnumber available properties, sellers often have the upper hand, able to set higher prices and even create bidding wars. Conversely, in a **buyer's market**, where supply exceeds demand, prices may fall, giving buyers more leverage.

Now, let's pause to review some core terms that will help you better navigate this complex but exciting world:

> **Appraisal** - A professional assessment of a property's market value, typically conducted by a

certified appraiser to help set a purchase price or determine financing options.

Closing Costs - Expenses associated with finalizing a real estate transaction, including fees for appraisal, title insurance, and legal services. These are due on the **Closing Date**.

Closing Date - The day when ownership transfers from the seller to the buyer, with all final documents signed and payments made.

Comparables (Comps) - Recently sold properties similar in size, location, and features to the one being evaluated, used to estimate fair market value.

Contingency - A condition in a purchase agreement that must be fulfilled for the sale to proceed, such as a satisfactory inspection or approved financing.

Deposit - Money placed by the buyer to secure the transaction. It's typically held in a **trust account** by a listing brokerage or the seller's lawyer if no realtor is used and is applied to the purchase price on the **Closing Date**.

Down Payment - An upfront portion of the purchase price, usually a percentage, applied toward a loan like a mortgage. The size of the down payment affects the loan amount and monthly payments.

Escrow - (U.S. term) A period where a neutral third party, the escrow agent, manages funds and documents until closing. In Canada, this role is handled by a **trust account** with the listing brokerage or seller's lawyer.

Equity - The share of the property's value that the owner holds outright, calculated as the property value minus any mortgage balance.

Lien - A legal claim against the property, serving as security for a debt. The property must be clear of liens before it can be sold.

Listing - A property put up for sale on the market, usually with details such as price, photos, and descriptions.

Market - The overall environment of real estate transactions, shaped by factors like supply, demand, and economic trends.

Mortgage - A loan used to purchase a property, with the property itself serving as collateral for the lender.

Offer - A proposal to purchase property at a specified price and under specific terms.

Title - The legal right to ownership of a property, documented and transferred at closing.

Title Insurance - Insurance protecting the buyer and lender from disputes over property ownership, often required in the U.S. and recommended in Canada.

Title Search - A review of public records to confirm legal ownership of a property and check for liens or claims.

Trust Account - A Canadian account where a listing brokerage or seller's lawyer holds the buyer's deposit until closing, similar to an escrow account in the U.S.

Armed with these definitions, you'll find it easier to understand the stages of a real estate transaction. Real estate cycles, much like waves, have peaks of high demand and prices followed by downturns where demand decreases, and prices stabilize or fall. Recognizing this cyclical nature helps you time your entry or exit from the market to align with your goals.

National real estate news may not reflect what's happening in your city or neighborhood. Market dynamics can vary significantly, with local trends often diverging from broader statistics. A national boom might not affect your area if local demand and development differ. By researching recent sale prices, time on the market, and local projects, you'll gain insights to make more informed decisions.

Real estate is rooted in numbers, but it's also highly personal. Buyers aren't just purchasing properties; they're investing in dreams, lifestyles, and futures. Sellers often feel connected to their homes and may value them beyond just market metrics. Understanding these emotional factors is invaluable for making grounded, empathetic decisions, whether negotiating or preparing to sell or buy. This foundation equips you to navigate the real estate market with confidence, helping you make the best possible decisions for your journey.

3: Tenant Basics for Beginners

Realtors often oversee leases, both residential and commercial; for this reason, I've included a section on self-representation as a tenant. In many regions where realtors are abundant and hungry for more business, realtors frequently manage residential tenancies. But once again—

this is not a legal requirement. Many rentals are offered directly by landlords, and even more tenants apply for leases independently, without realtor representation. For those in areas where realtors commonly manage rentals, this can create the impression that working with a realtor is necessary to secure a lease—while, in reality, it isn't.

This chapter is dedicated to empowering tenants to represent themselves in rental transactions and to know how to protect their interests as effectively as a realtor would. By managing lease agreements independently, tenants can gain valuable experience in navigating contracts and understanding their rights, building skills that will be valuable when the time comes to purchase their first property.

The first thing to do when representing yourself as a tenant is to understand the forms and legal standards that apply to your area. Start by researching the standard lease forms in your region—often available from your local real estate board. Look up terms like "lease agreement" or "agreement to lease," which will lead you to official forms that outline the standard conditions of a tenancy in your area. Using a standard lease form is crucial, as these documents are designed to meet regional legal requirements and include protections for both tenants and landlords.

Next, familiarize yourself with the tenancy laws that apply to your region. Search terms like "residential tenancy act" or "renters' rights in [your location]" to find governing documents that outline your rights and obligations as a tenant. These laws typically cover basic protections, such as the landlord's duty to provide a safe, habitable property and the tenant's responsibility to pay rent and maintain the property. Understanding these laws will help you navigate any issues that arise and ensure you're aware of your entitlements throughout your lease term.

When reviewing or preparing your lease, make sure it includes essential protections to secure your interests as a tenant. The lease should clearly specify the rent amount, payment due date, and any penalties for late payments, as well as the lease term (e.g., six months, one year, or month-to-month) with clear renewal or termination conditions. Ensure the terms for the security deposit are outlined, including the amount, where it will be held, and the conditions for its return. Maintenance responsibilities should be specified, with landlords typically handling major repairs and tenants responsible for daily upkeep. The lease should also outline the landlord's right to enter the property, with any required notice, and clarify which utilities or additional fees (e.g., water, gas) are covered by the landlord versus the tenant. Finally, check for early termination clauses and any penalties, which can provide flexibility should circumstances change.

Representing yourself as a tenant not only saves you potential realtor fees but also builds experience in managing legal agreements and understanding real estate fundamentals. This rental period serves as a financial and practical steppingstone, helping you save for a down payment and develop independence as you prepare for future homeownership. Renting may not be your ultimate goal, but using this time strategically can be a powerful investment in your future.

By representing yourself and focusing on saving where possible, you're actively preparing to move from tenant to homeowner. Every dollar you save now brings you closer to owning property and gaining the benefits of building equity. Approach this phase with a mindset of independence and preparation, knowing that the skills you develop will carry you into the next stage of your real estate journey.

I keep mentioning that you'll save on realtor fees, but *how* exactly, you might ask? After all, tenants don't usually pay realtor fees—those are covered by the landlord. But by representing yourself and approaching the listing agent or landlord directly, you can potentially save money by saving them money. Since the landlord doesn't have to pay a commission for your realtor (because you're unrepresented), consider politely suggesting that they pass some of those savings on to you. This could mean a rent discount for the first month or even a reduced rate throughout the lease term.

Everything is up for negotiation, and this may be your first chance to practice the art of negotiation—a skill that will be invaluable when it's time to buy your first home. Self-representation builds confidence and independence, allowing you to handle rental agreements on your terms while setting a solid foundation for your future in real estate. Every strategic decision you make as a tenant brings you closer to your goal of homeownership, equipping you with the tools and experience to succeed as you move forward in your real estate journey.

4: DIY Buying Guide

I'll sound like a broken record by the end of this book… but regardless, be advised that buying a home, whether it's your first property or part of a growing portfolio, doesn't require a realtor. With preparation and the right tools, you can confidently navigate the buying process on your own. In this chapter, we'll go through each stage—from organizing your finances to finding the perfect property and making a successful offer—with the goal of empowering you to make informed, independent decisions every step of the way.

The first step in buying a home is to know what you can afford. For most people (unless you're paying with cash), this means securing a loan (mortgage). Before even looking at properties, it's a good idea to get pre-approved for a mortgage. Pre-approval helps you set a realistic budget and shows sellers that you're a serious buyer. To do this, check your credit score, assess your finances, and reach out to lenders directly or through an online comparison platform to explore your options. Not all loans are the same, so take time to compare rates and terms. Whether you're looking at a conventional mortgage or exploring alternatives like FHA or VA loans, choosing the right financing is crucial. It's more than just finding the lowest interest rate—think about your budget, future plans, and even the neighborhood you hope to buy in. More information on mortgages and other financing options can be found in Chapter 7: Financing Made Simple.

Once you have a clear budget, it's time to define what you need versus what you want in a home. Maybe you know you need three bedrooms and a home office, but you'd like a backyard and a spacious kitchen. Clarifying these priorities early on makes the search process easier. With your list in hand, you're ready to start looking at properties. Today's real estate market is highly accessible, with websites that allow you to search listings directly without a realtor. In Canada, platforms like **Realtor.ca**, **Zolo**, and **HouseSigma** allow you to filter properties by price, size, location, and features. Sites like **Zillow** and **Realtor.com** offer similar options in the US. Sign up for alerts to get notifications when new listings match your criteria, so you don't miss out on a potential fit.

Keep in mind that these sites are typically connected to realtors at the other end of the contact page. When you fill out an online form for more details, you're often tagged as a "lead" for an agent to pursue for business, which may not be your intention. If you need more information, it's often better to contact the individual sellers or brokerages directly to avoid being followed up on by agents.

Also: when searching for a home, don't limit yourself to **MLS websites** (Multiple Listing Service websites). Owners of these properties are legally bound to real estate brokerages, making the listing agent your best point of contact for additional details. However, homes are also sold on public forums like **Kijiji**, **Facebook Marketplace**, and **Craigslist**—believe it or not. These properties are often called **FSBOs** (properties For Sale by Owner). FSBOs can also be found on **Purplebricks** in Canada, a site that lets sellers list properties independently. For these properties, the best contact is usually the owner or their representative, rather than a realtor, allowing for more direct communication.

When you find a property you like, it's time to make an offer. This can be the most intimidating part for many DIY buyers, but with some research, it's entirely manageable. Start by looking at recent sales in the area (comparable properties or: comps). Comps help you gauge the fair market value of the property, which is essential in crafting a reasonable offer. If the property has been on the market for a while, you may have more room to negotiate. On the other hand, in a hot market, you might need to offer close to the asking price—or even above it—to be competitive. Keep in mind that price isn't the only negotiable factor. You can include contingencies in your offer, such as financing or inspection contingencies, which give you an out if something doesn't go as planned. Submitting an offer without a realtor is straightforward; you can find standard offer forms online or consult a real estate attorney to review the offer before you submit it.

If your offer is accepted, congratulations—you're well on your way to owning your new home! But before you celebrate, there's one more essential step: the home inspection. Even if the home looks perfect, an inspection is critical to uncover any hidden issues that could cost you later on. Hire a qualified home inspector to evaluate the property's condition, from the roof to the foundation, and to identify any issues with systems like plumbing, electrical, and HVAC. If major issues come up, you can use the inspection report to negotiate repairs with the seller or even walk away if necessary.

Finally, it's time to close on the home. This is where all the paperwork comes together, and you officially become the owner. The closing process involves signing the final documents, transferring funds, and recording the deed. If this sounds complicated, don't worry. Title companies and real estate attorneys are there to guide you through, making sure everything is in order and that you understand each document before you sign. At the end of the closing, you'll receive the keys, and the property will officially be yours.

Buying a home on your own may sound challenging, but it's a rewarding experience that gives you full control over one of the biggest decisions of your life. By understanding each step in the process—from budgeting and researching to negotiating and closing—you'll feel empowered to make informed decisions without relying on a realtor. Whether you're buying for the first time or expanding your investments, the DIY approach to buying a home puts you in the driver's seat.

5: DIY Selling Guide

Selling a home might seem like a complex task best left to the experts, but the truth is, you can absolutely handle it on your own. By going the DIY route, you not only save on realtor commissions, but you also gain full control over the selling process, from prepping your home to negotiating the final sale. In this chapter, we'll explore every aspect of selling a home yourself, giving you the strategies and confidence to sell like a seasoned pro.

The first step to selling your home is to prepare it for the market, and a little effort can make a huge difference in attracting buyers. When buyers walk through the door, they need to be able to imagine themselves living in the space. Start by decluttering and depersonalizing your home—this means removing family photos, personal collections, and anything that distracts from the home's features. Aim for a clean, neutral look that allows buyers to envision their own lives there. Next, tackle any necessary repairs and give your home a deep clean. Fix leaky faucets, touch up paint, and make sure every room is spotless, especially high-traffic areas like the kitchen and bathrooms. A well-presented home signals to buyers that the property has been well cared for and is move-in ready, which can increase its appeal.

Have you heard the term "staging"? All it really means is making your home look inviting and presentable for potential buyers. You don't need a professional stager; small adjustments can make a big impact. Rearrange furniture to create a spacious feel, add simple touches like fresh flowers or a cozy throw, and stick to neutral colors to appeal to a wider audience. And don't forget about "curb appeal"—that's how good your house looks from the street, or the overall impression of the exterior. Make sure it's neat and welcoming by mowing the lawn, trimming bushes, and maybe adding a fresh coat of paint to the front door. The goal is a strong first impression that invites buyers to see more.

Once your home is looking its best, it's time to set the right price. Pricing a home correctly is one of the most important factors in a successful sale. Start by researching comparable sales in your area, known as "comps," to get a sense of what similar homes are selling for. Pay attention to homes with similar square footage, location, and condition, as these factors heavily influence a property's value. Setting a realistic price is key; if you price too high, you risk scaring off potential buyers, and if you price too low, you may leave money on the table. It can be tempting to overprice in hopes of negotiating down, but buyers are savvy and will often skip listings that seem overpriced from the start. By setting a fair, competitive price, you'll attract more interest and increase your chances of a faster sale.

With your home priced and ready to show, the next step is marketing. Today, most buyers start their search online, which means high-quality photos are essential. Consider hiring a professional photographer to capture your home in the best light, or, if you're doing it yourself, use natural light and take wide-angle shots to showcase each room's space. Write a compelling listing description that highlights your home's best features, like an upgraded kitchen, a spacious backyard, or proximity to schools and amenities. The listing is your chance to tell a story about your home, so use language that appeals to potential buyers. Once you have the photos and description, list your home on popular real estate websites and social media platforms. The more visibility your listing has, the more potential buyers you'll reach.

If you're comfortable with it, hosting your own open house is a great way to attract multiple buyers at once. Choose a time that's convenient for potential buyers, like a weekend afternoon, and create a welcoming atmosphere. Make sure the home is clean, bright, and free from any strong odors.

Offer refreshments and be prepared to answer questions about the home, the neighborhood, and any recent updates you've made. An open house not only shows off the property, but it also gives buyers a chance to envision themselves living there, which can help create a stronger connection to the home.

As offers start coming in, it's time to put on your negotiation hat. When reviewing offers, don't just focus on the price—consider other terms like the closing date, contingencies, and whether the buyer has been pre-approved for a mortgage. If an offer is lower than expected, you can always counter with a higher price or request different terms. Be prepared for some back-and-forth, and don't hesitate to negotiate items other than price, like repairs or closing costs. The goal is to find an agreement that works for both parties and allows you to walk away satisfied.

Once you accept an offer, the sale moves into the closing phase. This is where all the paperwork is finalized, funds are transferred, and the title officially changes hands. You'll need to sign a closing statement that outlines all the costs involved in the transaction, as well as other documents like the deed and tax forms. If the closing process sounds daunting, don't worry, companies and real estate attorneys are there to help ensure everything is handled properly. At the end of the closing, you'll hand over the keys, and the sale will be complete.

Selling a home on your own may seem like a lot of work, but with the right approach, it's entirely manageable—and rewarding. From preparing and pricing your home to marketing it effectively and handling offers, you have all the tools you need to sell like a pro. By taking charge of the process, you'll not only save money but also gain valuable experience and confidence as a DIY seller. And who knows? You might even enjoy the journey.

6: Closing the Deal

Closing on a property is an exciting step, marking the moment when ownership officially transfers from seller to buyer. But before you get the keys, there are essential steps and protections in place to ensure a smooth and secure transaction. These final processes involve a series of agreements, verifications, and checks that ultimately protect both parties. In the U.S., you'll often hear the term **escrow** to describe the period between signing the purchase agreement and the closing date. Let's walk through what this means, why it matters, and what to expect in the closing process, including title insurance and the role of a lawyer.

Once the buyer and seller have signed the purchase agreement, the property enters what's known in the U.S. as "escrow." This is a holding period where a neutral third party, often an escrow agent or company, safeguards the transaction details. This agent securely holds items like the buyer's deposit, critical documents, and funds, ensuring that all conditions of the sale are met before finalizing the transaction. For example, if the buyer needs to secure financing or the seller must complete specific repairs, the escrow agent verifies each requirement before releasing funds and documents to complete the sale.

In Canada, the approach differs slightly. When using a realtor, the listing brokerage often holds the buyer's deposit in a trust account until closing. However, for sellers choosing the DIY route and opting out of a realtor's services, a similar function can be achieved independently. In these cases, a lawyer typically steps in to handle the escrow-like duties, holding the deposit and ensuring that conditions are met. The lawyer will manage the buyer's deposit, track the transaction's requirements, and confirm that all terms are satisfied before funds change hands. This escrow-like process may also apply in other countries that do not use formal escrow agents.

In DIY transactions, especially for sellers, having a lawyer's support is essential to ensure that the sale proceeds smoothly without the brokerage's usual involvement. The lawyer holds the deposit, confirms the completion of all required conditions, and protects both buyer and seller by coordinating communication, document verification, and fund release. For example, if the purchase agreement includes contingencies like inspections or repair commitments, the lawyer monitors these requirements, releasing funds only once all conditions are fulfilled. This approach ensures that both parties meet their obligations before the sale closes.

During this time, the lawyer's role also extends to conducting or supervising a **title search**. This critical step confirms the ownership history and ensures there are no outstanding claims, liens, or legal issues that could affect the buyer's ownership rights after closing. Title searches vary depending on the property's location and history, but they generally involve a detailed examination of public records, past deeds, and any legal filings related to the property. By confirming a "clean title"—meaning the property is free from disputes or unpaid debts—the lawyer prevents future complications and assures the buyer that their ownership is secure.

In addition to the title search, most buyers choose or are required to purchase **title insurance**. Title insurance is a one-time premium that protects both the buyer and the lender against unforeseen title issues that may surface after the sale, such as a previously unreported lien or a challenge to the property's ownership. While the title search is thorough, title insurance provides an extra layer of security, ensuring that if a claim does arise, the buyer and lender are financially protected. This insurance essentially guarantees that the buyer's ownership rights are fully protected, providing peace of mind against potential future claims.

As the closing date approaches, the lawyer in a DIY transaction coordinates with the buyer, seller, and lender to confirm that all necessary steps are completed. This includes verifying that the buyer's funds are prepared, that the property title is clear, and that both parties have signed all required documents. The lawyer also prepares a **closing statement**—a document outlining all financial aspects of the transaction, from the purchase price to any fees and taxes. Reviewing this statement closely ensures transparency, avoiding surprises on closing day.

On the day of closing, all parties typically meet to sign the final paperwork. This includes signing the closing statement, transferring the deed, and completing any last-minute verifications. Once everything is signed, the lawyer releases the funds to the seller, and the buyer receives the deed, legally transferring ownership. This moment officially completes the transaction, and the buyer can finally claim keys and call the property their own.

Although the closing process can seem complex, each step is designed to ensure that the buyer's new ownership is secure and that both parties are fully protected. By understanding escrow or similar arrangements, title insurance, and the roles lawyers play, you'll be ready to navigate these final steps with clarity and confidence, bringing you closer to completing your real estate journey on your terms.

7: Financing Made Simple

Financing is the foundation of any real estate transaction, whether you're buying a home to live in or investing in property. Knowing how to secure financing, which options are available, and how to budget for the true costs of homeownership will help you make informed, confident decisions. In this chapter, we'll cover everything you need to know about financing, from understanding your mortgage options to exploring alternative financing methods if traditional loans aren't the right fit.

Before you start searching for a property, it's essential to assess your budget and understand what you can realistically afford. Financing usually begins with checking your credit score. Your credit score plays a big role in determining the types of loans available to you and the interest rate you're likely to receive. A higher score generally means better loan terms, while a lower score may limit your options. If you're planning to buy soon, taking a few months to improve your credit by paying off outstanding debts or correcting any errors on your report can save you money in the long term. With your credit in good shape, the next step is to get pre-approved for a mortgage. Pre-approval gives you a clear budget to work with and shows sellers that you're a serious buyer. This step is straightforward: you'll provide a lender with information on your income, assets, debts, and credit score, and they'll issue a pre-approval letter stating how much they're willing to lend you.

Once you know your budget, it's time to explore mortgage options. In both Canada and the U.S., conventional mortgages are the most common choice for homebuyers, usually requiring a higher credit score and down payment. In the U.S., a conventional loan often requires around 20%

down to avoid private mortgage insurance (PMI). In Canada, a 20% down payment also allows buyers to bypass mortgage insurance. However, for buyers needing lower down payment options, there are programs in both countries designed to help.

In the U.S., FHA loans backed by the Federal Housing Administration offer an accessible option with down payments as low as 3.5%, making them popular with first-time buyers and those with lower credit scores. In Canada, a similar option is the CMHC Insured Mortgage (or through private insurers like Sagen or Canada Guaranty), which allows qualified buyers to purchase a home with as little as 5% down on properties under $500,000. Both FHA and CMHC options involve mortgage insurance premiums, which add to the monthly payment but can make homeownership more accessible.

Understanding the different types of lenders in Canada can also guide you in your decision. Canadian lenders are classified as A, B, or C lenders based on qualification criteria. A-lenders, which include major banks and credit unions, offer the best rates but have stricter requirements, generally suited for borrowers with stable income, good credit, and a sufficient down payment. B-lenders, which include alternative lenders, are more flexible with credit scores or income verification but charge higher interest rates. Lastly, C-lenders are private lenders who provide the most flexible terms, often catering to borrowers who might not qualify with other lenders but at the highest interest rates.

You'll also encounter the choice between a **fixed-rate** and a **variable-rate** (or adjustable-rate) mortgage. A fixed-rate mortgage locks in an interest rate for the loan term, offering stability in monthly payments—a common choice when rates are low, and borrowers want predictability. A variable or adjustable-rate mortgage, on the other hand, has interest rates that fluctuate with market conditions, which can result in lower payments initially but may rise or fall over time, impacting your monthly payments. Deciding between the two depends on your financial situation, comfort with potential rate changes, and long-term goals.

As a general guideline, you can estimate how much home you might afford by multiplying your total annual income by 4, though this is a rough calculation and often inaccurate. The most reliable way to determine your budget is through mortgage pre-approval, which takes into account your credit history, income stability, and down payment, giving you a clear picture of what you can realistically afford.

For current homeowners looking to expand their portfolio, home equity loans or home equity lines of credit (HELOCs) are viable options for financing additional real estate investments. A home equity loan allows you to borrow against the equity you've built in your home, providing a lump sum that's repaid over time. Alternatively, a HELOC works more like a credit card, giving you access to funds up to a certain limit, which you can draw from as needed. Both options let you leverage your existing property's value to fund new investments, offering flexibility as you grow your real estate holdings.

Financing might feel like the most technical part of the buying process, but it's a crucial step that sets the foundation for a successful real estate journey. By understanding mortgage types, loan terms, and alternative financing options, you'll be well-prepared to secure the funding you need. The process might seem complicated, but each choice—whether it's a loan type, rate structure, or budgeting decision—brings you closer to your goal. With a clear plan and the right resources, you're ready to navigate the financing process confidently and make one of the biggest financial investments of your life.

8: Negotiation Tactics

Negotiating in real estate is both an art and a skill, and it can make a substantial difference in the outcome of your transaction. Whether you're buying, selling, or investing, a strong negotiation strategy helps you secure the best possible terms and price, while also giving you confidence in your choices. In this chapter, we'll explore essential tactics to navigate negotiations, handle counteroffers, and find solutions that work for all parties involved.

One of the most important factors in any negotiation is understanding the current market conditions. For buyers, a buyer's market—where there are more homes for sale than there are buyers—can create leverage to negotiate for lower prices or request concessions from the seller. In contrast, a seller's market—where demand exceeds supply—gives sellers a stronger position, often allowing them to price higher and receive multiple offers. For a seller, knowing your market's status can help you set a competitive price or, in favorable conditions, position your property to attract the best possible offers. By understanding these conditions, both buyers and sellers can adapt their approach and set realistic expectations.

When it comes to setting an initial offer or price, data-driven strategies are among the most effective. Buyers should start by researching comparable sales, or comps, in the area. Looking at recent sales of similar properties will give you insight into fair market value, which will help you craft a reasonable starting offer. If the property is priced significantly above comps, you'll have a strong basis to negotiate a lower price. Conversely, if it's priced fairly or even below market value, you may choose to offer closer to the asking price, especially in competitive markets where quick action is essential.

For sellers, understanding comps is equally critical. Setting an attractive yet profitable asking price requires aligning with market trends and positioning your property to catch the interest of serious buyers. A well-researched price gives you leverage in negotiations by showing that the property is valued reasonably in the current market. This strategy can bring in competitive offers while avoiding the pitfall of overpricing, which could drive away potential buyers.

For buyers, including contingencies in your offer can be a powerful negotiation tool. Contingencies are conditions that must be met for the sale to go forward, such as a satisfactory home inspection or confirmed financing. Contingencies provide essential protection, allowing you to back out or renegotiate if unexpected issues arise. A home inspection contingency, for instance, gives you the leverage to request repairs or a price reduction if significant problems are discovered. However, in competitive markets, you'll want to be cautious about including too many contingencies, as they may make your offer less attractive to the seller. The key is to use contingencies strategically, protecting your interests while keeping your offer appealing.

Timing plays a significant role in real estate negotiations. If a property has been on the market for an extended period, the seller may be more willing to accept a lower offer or consider additional requests. For sellers, this means being aware of the impact of timing on buyer interest and possibly adjusting expectations if a property doesn't sell as quickly as anticipated. On the other hand, newly listed properties, especially in popular areas, are likely to attract more interest and competition. As a buyer, acting quickly and decisively when you find a home you love can make a big difference, while as a seller, strategically listing your property can help you maximize interest and the quality of offers received. Understanding timing and the seller's motivation—such as a need to move quickly due to job relocation or family circumstances—can help both parties tailor their approach for more favorable terms.

Handling counteroffers is another critical skill in any negotiation, whether you're buying or selling. If a seller responds to your initial offer with a counteroffer, it's essential to review it carefully. Take time to consider which terms are non-negotiable and where you might be flexible. For example, you may be open to adjusting the closing date or minor repairs but remain firm on the price. Thoughtfully responding to counteroffers can often lead to common ground without compromising your primary goals. For sellers, responding to a buyer's counteroffer may involve minor price adjustments or offering to cover specific closing costs. This flexibility allows you to reach an agreement while keeping the deal aligned with your priorities. The goal for both sides is to approach counter offers thoughtfully, making concessions where possible and staying clear on essential priorities.

Throughout the negotiation process, remember that the best outcomes come from a collaborative, problem-solving mindset. Real estate negotiations aren't about winning or losing; rather, they're about reaching an agreement that satisfies both parties. Listening to the other side's needs can make a significant difference in the tone and success of the negotiation. For example, if a buyer requests certain repairs or upgrades, a seller might find a compromise by offering credit toward repairs rather than completing them before the sale. Approaching negotiations with a solutions-focused perspective creates a more positive environment that often leads to successful deals for both sides.

Patience and professionalism are two of the most powerful tools you can bring to any negotiation. Real estate transactions can be emotional, but staying calm and composed allows you to make rational, well-informed decisions. Avoid impulsive choices, such as agreeing to uncomfortable terms just to close quickly and take time to evaluate each offer or counteroffer carefully. As a buyer or seller, don't hesitate to consult a real estate lawyer if you have questions or need guidance on specific terms. Being patient shows you're committed to finding the right deal and willing to wait for terms that align with your objectives.

Negotiation is a skill that develops with experience, and each transaction will build your confidence in advocating for your interests. By entering negotiations prepared with data, a flexible mindset, and a clear sense of your priorities, you'll be well-prepared to handle offers and counter offers with ease. The goal is to achieve a transaction that aligns with your vision, bringing you one step closer to reaching your real estate dreams.

9: DIY Investing

Investing in real estate is one of the most powerful ways to build wealth, and the beauty of it is that you don't need a professional to get started. By taking a DIY approach, you have the freedom to select properties that align with your goals, make strategic decisions about improvements, and take control over how your investment grows. In this chapter, we'll explore the fundamentals of real estate investing, from finding the right property to managing it effectively, and we'll walk through essential strategies that can help you turn real estate into a lucrative part of your financial future.

Before diving in, it's essential to get clear on your investment goals. Real estate investing comes in many forms, and your objectives will shape the type of property you choose and the strategies you employ. Are you looking for a rental property that provides steady income, or are you interested in flipping properties for a faster return? Perhaps you're considering commercial properties, which can offer long-term, stable tenants but may require a higher initial investment. By defining your goals upfront, you set the stage for decisions that align with your vision and financial plans.

Once you know your goals, the next step is finding the right property. Start by researching areas with strong demand, as this will impact both property value and rental potential. For rental properties, look for neighborhoods with job growth, quality schools, and amenities that attract long-term renters. If you're considering a property to flip, look for homes in emerging neighborhoods where values are on the rise but property prices are still reasonable. Regardless of the type, conducting a market analysis of recent comparable sales— also known as "comps"—helps you understand what similar properties are selling for and ensures you don't overpay. In the DIY approach, thorough research is your best tool for making a smart purchase.

When you find a property that meets your criteria, budgeting becomes crucial. Real estate investments come with costs beyond the purchase price, including property taxes, insurance, maintenance, and potential renovations. For rental properties, plan for regular upkeep, as maintaining a property helps retain tenants and protect your investment's value. If you're considering flipping, factor in the cost of repairs and improvements, along with a buffer for unexpected expenses. Setting a realistic budget that accounts for all these factors keeps your investment manageable and increases the likelihood of a profitable outcome.

Managing a rental property yourself requires commitment but can be highly rewarding. Start by selecting reliable tenants through a screening process that includes background checks, income verification, and references. Good tenants are one of your greatest assets, as they ensure a steady cash flow and help keep maintenance costs down. Establishing a lease agreement with clear terms on rent, responsibilities, and expectations can prevent misunderstandings and make your role as a landlord smoother. Communication is key—promptly addressing tenant requests and staying on top of property maintenance can make a positive impact, increasing tenant retention and, ultimately, your return on investment.

If you're interested in flipping properties, project management skills are just as important as financial planning. A successful flip requires overseeing contractors, budgeting for materials, and keeping the renovation timeline on track. Small upgrades, like fresh paint, updated fixtures, and landscaping, can increase a property's value significantly. However, if you're aiming for a major renovation, focus on improvements that offer the highest return, like kitchen and bathroom upgrades. Timing is crucial, too—completing renovations during peak market seasons, when buyers are actively searching, increases your chances of selling quickly and for a higher price.

Alternative strategies, like short-term rentals, can also offer strong returns, particularly in popular tourist areas. Platforms like Airbnb and Booking.com allow you to rent out properties on a short-term basis, which can be profitable if demand is high. However, short-term rentals require frequent cleaning, regular management, and compliance with local regulations, so they may not be ideal for everyone. If you're considering this option, research your area's rules on short-term rentals to ensure you're operating legally and profitably.

As your investment portfolio grows, diversification is another consideration. By investing in different types of properties—residential, commercial, or even multi-family—you reduce the impact of market fluctuations on your overall portfolio. Diversification can help stabilize your income and offer new opportunities, like moving from residential to commercial or expanding into different regions. Each property type has its own unique benefits and risks, so consider how they align with your goals and risk tolerance. Diversifying within real estate adds strength to your portfolio, creating multiple income streams while building long-term wealth.

Real estate investment is as much about mindset as it is about numbers. Patience, resilience, and a willingness to adapt are essential traits. Markets change, tenants come and go, and unexpected repairs happen. By approaching each investment with a clear plan, realistic budget, and commitment to learning, you're better equipped to handle the ups and downs of real estate. The DIY approach offers unmatched flexibility and control, allowing you to shape your investments in ways that fit your lifestyle and ambitions.

Taking a DIY approach to real estate investing isn't just about saving money on commissions or fees; it's about creating a direct path to financial independence. With a clear strategy, careful research, and hands-on management, you're ready to make real estate a dynamic and rewarding part of your financial journey. Embrace the process, stay informed, and remember that each decision brings you closer to your goals, building wealth and freedom on your own terms.

10: Risk Management

Every investment carries risk, and real estate is no exception. However, one of the advantages of real estate is that, with a little planning, many of these risks can be managed or even minimized. By understanding common risks in the real estate world, you'll be better equipped to protect your investment, make informed decisions, and prepare for challenges that may arise. This chapter will help you recognize these potential risks and guide you through practical strategies to manage them effectively, so you can move forward with confidence.

One of the most common risks in real estate is market risk, which comes from the possibility that property values or rental demand may decrease. Market conditions are influenced by a variety of factors, including the local economy, employment rates, and population trends. For example, if a major employer in an area downsizes or relocates, housing demand could drop, leading to lower property values. To protect yourself, research the market carefully before buying, paying particular attention to areas with stable economic activity, growing job markets, and infrastructure developments that suggest long-term growth potential. Investing in areas with diverse economies reduces the chance that a downturn in one industry will significantly impact property values, giving you a buffer against this type of risk.

Property-specific risks are another aspect to consider, as they relate to issues with the condition, location, or type of property you're purchasing. These risks can vary widely, from unexpected maintenance costs to potential environmental hazards. One of the best ways to manage this is by conducting a thorough property inspection before you buy. A qualified inspector can identify structural issues, outdated electrical systems, plumbing problems, and more. Addressing these problems early on allows you to factor repair costs into your budget or negotiate a lower purchase price. Additionally, if you're investing in certain property types, like multi-family buildings or commercial properties, understand that these often come with different challenges and maintenance needs. Preparing for property-specific risks helps you avoid unpleasant surprises and protects your bottom line.

For rental property owners, tenant-related risks are part of managing real estate. This can include everything from problem tenants who fail to pay rent to periods of vacancy that result in lost income. To mitigate tenant risk, start with a thorough screening process that includes background checks, income verification, and references. A good tenant is a valuable asset, as they're more likely to pay on time, treat the property with respect, and stay for a longer term. Vacancy risk is also worth considering. High turnover can be costly, especially if your property sits empty for an extended period. To avoid this, consider investing in properties in areas with strong rental demand and setting a rental price that's competitive yet profitable. Good tenants and consistent demand are crucial for steady cash flow, making your rental investment more reliable.

Another important factor in risk management is liquidity, which refers to how easily you can access your money if needed. Real estate is generally less liquid than other investments, meaning you can't quickly sell a property to free up cash. If you find yourself in a position where you need to sell quickly, you might have to accept a lower price than expected. To manage this risk, maintain a cash reserve as a financial safety net. This reserve can cover mortgage payments or repairs in case of a vacancy, ensuring you're not forced to sell under pressure. By planning for liquidity needs, you'll have more flexibility and security if circumstances change unexpectedly.

Interest rate risk is another consideration, particularly if you're using financing to purchase a property. When interest rates rise, so do monthly mortgage payments on adjustable-rate mortgages, which can affect cash flow and profitability. If you're concerned about rate increases, consider locking in a fixed-rate mortgage, which guarantees a steady payment throughout the loan term. For those with existing adjustable-rate mortgages, refinancing into a fixed-rate loan during periods of low rates may be a smart move. Keeping an eye on interest rates and considering their impact on your investments can help you prepare for potential changes in the market.

Legal risks are also worth addressing, as they can become costly and complicated if not managed properly. Real estate transactions involve contracts, lease agreements, and local regulations that must be followed carefully. For example, if you're renting out a property, landlord-tenant laws govern everything from lease agreements to eviction processes. Familiarize yourself with these laws to avoid legal disputes and fines. Documentation is key; keep records of all interactions with tenants, maintenance requests, and any updates you make to the property. In the event of a dispute, thorough documentation can be invaluable. Consulting with a real estate attorney for complex matters or simply to review legal documents can also provide extra protection, ensuring you're in compliance and prepared for any challenges that may arise.

When navigating the complexities of real estate transactions, understanding your legal rights and obligations is essential to managing risk effectively. While this book provides tools to help you approach real estate independently, certain situations may still benefit from professional legal advice. If you encounter uncertainties about specific laws, contractual terms, or your rights as a buyer, seller, or landlord, consulting a real estate lawyer can offer clarity and protection. Though legal fees can vary, they may still cost less than hiring a realtor, depending on the scope of your needs. Always inquire about fees upfront to make an informed decision that balances both independence and security.

Overall, successful real estate investing isn't about avoiding risk entirely—it's about managing it wisely. By identifying potential risks upfront and implementing practical solutions, you'll create a strong foundation for your investments. Whether it's through detailed property inspections, proper tenant screening, or securing a fixed-rate mortgage, each step you take towards minimizing risk brings you closer to achieving your real estate goals with confidence and stability. Understanding and managing risk transforms challenges into opportunities, allowing you to build wealth in a secure, informed way.

11: Winning with DIY

Real estate is a universal language, and the journey of buying, selling, or investing in property can look very different depending on where you are in the world. In this chapter, we'll explore inspiring stories from individuals who took a DIY approach to real estate and achieved their goals—whether they were buying their first home, selling a property, or investing in a rental portfolio. Each story highlights the strategies they used, the challenges they faced, and the lessons they learned along the way.

Priya, a first-time homebuyer in Toronto, Canada, took on the competitive real estate market with determination, opting for a DIY approach instead of hiring a realtor. She attended open houses, researched neighborhoods, and secured pre-approval for her mortgage. After months of searching, Priya found a condo in a neighborhood she loved. She negotiated directly with the seller, using recent comparable sales to support her offer, and worked with a real estate attorney to finalize the purchase agreement. In the end, Priya bought her first home without paying realtor fees, achieving her goal of homeownership independently.

Jason, a Seattle-based software engineer, decided to sell his condo himself after receiving a job relocation offer. With Seattle's hot market, he felt confident that he could manage the sale without a realtor. Jason prepared his home by decluttering, staging, and taking professional-quality photos, then listed it on real estate websites and social media. Within a week, he received multiple offers, one of which was above asking price. After working with a real estate attorney to handle the paperwork, Jason closed the sale smoothly and saved tens of thousands of dollars in commissions.

Carlos, a Filipino-Canadian investor, was drawn to the growing tourist destinations in Cebu and Boracay. Initially, he planned to purchase beachfront land, but he soon discovered that, as he was no longer a Filipino citizen, he was restricted from owning land and limited to buying only condominium units. Adjusting his strategy, Carlos purchased two condo units in Cebu and transformed them into vacation rentals. With the help of a local property manager, he successfully marketed the condos to international tourists on platforms like Airbnb, and his rental income has since exceeded his expectations, creating a steady income stream from his investment.

Sophie and Mark, a couple from New Brunswick, Canada, had always dreamed of flipping homes. They started by purchasing a small, outdated bungalow in a neighborhood showing signs of growth. Working with a tight budget, they focused on high-impact upgrades that would add the most resale value: repainting, updating the kitchen, and modernizing the bathroom. They managed the project themselves, carefully researching materials and hiring contractors only for essential work. After several months of hard work, they listed the home for sale and received multiple offers, eventually closing at a price well above their initial expectations.

Mia, a teacher from Austin, Texas, turned to real estate to build a steady rental income. She started with a modest investment, purchasing a duplex in an area with strong rental demand. Mia chose to live in one unit and rent out the other, which helped offset her mortgage payments. Over time, she was able to save for a second rental property. Now, Mia continues to manage her properties herself, taking a hands-on approach with tenants and daily property needs.

These case studies showcase the diverse paths individuals can take to succeed in real estate, whether it's buying, selling, or investing. Priya, Jason, Carlos, Mia, and Sophie and Mark each faced unique challenges and tailored their approaches to meet their goals, saving on commissions and gaining valuable experience. From negotiating a first home purchase to flipping properties, house hacking, and managing vacation rentals, their stories demonstrate that with determination, research, and resourcefulness, anyone can navigate the real estate market independently and achieve meaningful financial growth on their own terms.

As you embark on your journey, remember that these strategies can be adapted to fit your unique path in real estate. Whether buying, selling, or investing, embrace each step with confidence, and soon, you'll be crafting your own success story.

12: Empowered Futures

The real estate market is continuously evolving, shaped by trends in technology, economics, and lifestyle changes. As you plan your next steps, it's helpful to understand where the market is heading and how you can align your DIY real estate journey with these future shifts. This chapter will explore key trends and emerging opportunities in real estate, helping you prepare to adapt, grow, and make the most of what's ahead.

One significant trend is the shifting demand for different types of spaces due to changes in lifestyle and work habits. The rise of remote work has changed where and how people live, as they no longer need to be near traditional office hubs. Smaller cities, suburban areas, and even rural locations are seeing increased demand as people look for more space, lower costs, and lifestyle flexibility. For investors, this creates new opportunities to explore markets beyond major metropolitan areas. Investing in regions with lower property costs and high potential for appreciation, especially in areas gaining popularity among remote workers, could be highly rewarding. Staying informed about these shifts will allow you to identify emerging markets and make timely investment decisions.

Technology continues to transform the real estate landscape, making it more accessible and efficient for buyers, sellers, and investors alike. Virtual tours and 3D staging tools, like Matterport and iGUIDE, have become popular, allowing buyers to explore properties remotely—a trend accelerated by the pandemic. For DIY sellers, these tools offer a unique advantage, helping you reach buyers who may not be able to visit in person and providing a competitive edge. Additionally, real estate apps have revolutionized how people search for and manage properties. In the U.S., platforms like Zillow, Redfin, and Trulia offer robust search tools, while in Canada, Realtor.ca, HouseSigma, and Zolo provide similar functionality. For rental management, apps like Avail and Cozy help property owners screen tenants, collect rent, and track expenses from a single platform. Embracing these tools can streamline your process and make your real estate management more efficient.

Another major trend shaping the future of real estate is the emphasis on sustainable and smart properties. Buyers and renters increasingly seek homes that are energy-efficient and environmentally friendly. Features like solar panels, energy-saving appliances, and smart thermostats are not only attractive to environmentally-conscious buyers but can also lower utility costs, making them a strong investment in the long term. As an investor, considering properties with these features, or upgrading existing properties to include them, could enhance your property's market appeal. "Smart home" technology—such as security systems, automated lighting, and voice-activated controls—has also become a major selling point, particularly among younger buyers. Integrating sustainable and smart features into your properties can increase rental demand and boost resale values as these preferences continue to grow.

Beyond traditional property ownership, alternative real estate investments are on the rise. REITs, or Real Estate Investment Trusts, allow you to invest in real estate without directly purchasing a property, often in areas like commercial real estate or large developments. This provides diversification and a more hands-off approach for those interested in real estate but hesitant to manage a property. Another emerging option is fractional ownership, which allows multiple investors to buy shares in a property. This approach can make high-value properties accessible to smaller investors, opening doors to upscale or high-demand markets. Additionally, international real estate investment is gaining popularity, especially as remote work enables more people to live in diverse locations. Investing in international markets can diversify your portfolio and offer unique appreciation opportunities, although it does require thorough research and familiarity with local laws.

Economic and social factors will also influence the real estate market in the coming years. Interest rates, inflation, and economic policy shifts can all affect home values and rental demand. Generational trends, such as the increasing number of millennial and Gen Z buyers entering the market, are shaping demand for smaller homes, flexible living arrangements, and affordable urban options. As more younger buyers prioritize experiences and lifestyle over large properties, smaller, more efficient spaces are gaining traction. Investors who understand these preferences can make strategic choices about property types and locations, ensuring they meet the needs of a changing demographic landscape.

Lastly, blockchain technology is an area to watch, as it has the potential to bring new transparency and efficiency to real estate transactions. Blockchain can facilitate faster, more secure transactions through smart contracts—digitally enforced agreements that automatically execute when predefined conditions are met. This technology could streamline everything from property transfers to ownership verification, especially in international transactions. Although still in its early stages, staying informed about blockchain advancements could give you an advantage if and when it becomes more widely adopted in the industry.

As you look ahead, remember that the future of real estate is rich with potential. Embracing new technologies, adapting to shifting market demands, and exploring innovative investment options will keep you agile and ready for whatever comes next. Each decision you make brings you closer to a more empowered future, allowing you to build a real estate portfolio that adapts, grows, and endures.

Real estate is more than just an investment; it's a journey toward financial independence, adaptability, and growth. By understanding future trends and staying open to new opportunities, you'll continue to strengthen your position and create a legacy that reflects your personal vision. Keep learning, keep adapting, and keep moving forward—each step you take is building a future shaped entirely by you.

13: Final Thoughts

From the very beginning, my purpose in writing this book was to share the knowledge and tools to help you take control of your real estate journey. Real estate can seem overwhelming and costly, often feeling like a world reserved for those with insider knowledge or endless resources. But I believe that everyone has the right to participate in this journey, to build wealth, and to find financial independence on their terms.

The beauty of DIY real estate is not just in saving money—though that's certainly a powerful motivator—but in empowering yourself to make confident, informed decisions that directly impact your life and your future. By choosing to go the DIY route, you're choosing independence, knowledge, and the satisfaction of seeing what you're truly capable of.

Real estate is one of the most significant financial decisions many of us will make, and every choice you make along the way is a step toward shaping your future. Each dollar saved on commissions or fees is one that you retain—an amount that can be reinvested, used to enrich your lifestyle, or set aside for other dreams. The power of DIY real estate lies in reclaiming those resources, keeping them within your control.

While this journey is built on independence, remember that support is available whenever you need it. If you ever feel uncertain about the legal aspects of a transaction or have questions about your rights, consulting a real estate lawyer can offer valuable peace of mind. Legal fees vary, and while some may be comparable to realtor commissions, they might also be less—making it worthwhile to ask about costs before committing. This added layer of protection can help you feel fully prepared as you work toward your real estate goals with confidence.

Throughout this book, I've aimed to break down the process into manageable steps, making real estate as accessible as possible for anyone, regardless of experience. Real estate doesn't have to be exclusive or reserved for experts; it's something everyone can navigate with the right approach and a willingness to learn. By taking this journey, you're not only saving money but also cultivating a sense of ownership and confidence that extends beyond real estate and into all areas of your life.

Now, it's your turn to take what you've learned and put it into action. Start where you feel most comfortable—whether that's exploring a new neighborhood for a potential home, preparing your property for sale, or researching rental opportunities. Remember, every decision, no matter how small, brings you closer to your goals. The path may not always be easy, but the rewards—both financial and personal—are worth every step.

If there's one message I hope you carry forward, it's that real estate is as much about independence and self-belief as it is about wealth-building. Embrace the learning process, stay resilient in the face of challenges, and celebrate each milestone. You are more than capable of shaping your real estate story and turning your goals into reality.

Thank you for allowing me to be a part of your journey. Now, go out there, take action, and make your real estate dreams come to life.